JAZZ STANDARDS
FOR ★ UKULELE

ISBN 978-1-4950-0928-0

Hal ● LEONARD®
CORPORATION
7777 W. BLUEMOUND RD. P.O. BOX 13819 MILWAUKEE, WI 53213

Visit Hal Leonard Online at
www.halleonard.com

HOW TO PLAY MOUTH TRUMPET

Playing the ukulele is even more fun when you add the melody on trumpet—using only your voice! **Mouth trumpet** (also called "lip trumpet" or "human trumpet") is a vocal technique that anyone can learn with practice. It first became popular during the 1920s, but has recently made a major comeback. Artists incorporating mouth trumpet into their music include Cliff Edwards ("Ukulele Ike"), Harry Mills (of The Mills Brothers), Earl Okin, Denise Reis, Lawrence "Lipbone" Redding, Victoria Vox and Yancarlos Sanchez.

To produce a trumpet sound with your voice, follow these steps:

- First, sing the notes using a "dee" syllable. Your tongue will momentarily stop the pitch when making the consonant sounds behind your front teeth. (Don't stretch your mouth into a smile—keep your lips relaxed.)

- Next, close your lips and practice simply blowing air through a small opening in one side of your mouth. Your teeth should be held slightly apart.

- Use your tongue to make "d" consonants while you're blowing air. This will create a natural "puffing" effect.

- Here's the fun (and tricky) part! Sing the notes using "dee" at the same time you're blowing air through the side of your mouth. The tone will change depending on how tightly your lips are closed. Experiment to find the right balance of lip tension and air flow.

TIP: Some people get better results by blowing air through the center of their lips instead of the side. Regardless, try not to twist or pucker your lips.

Once you've mastered the basic technique, try adding vibrato like you would with your singing voice. If you know how to roll your tongue or "flutter" your lips, you can also incorporate those as special effects. Listen to recordings by the artists listed above, and keep practicing to refine your technique and style.

Your mouth trumpet will have a unique sound, just like your speaking and singing voice. Find yours and strum along!

CONTENTS

Ac-cent-tchu-ate the Positive

from the Motion Picture HERE COME THE WAVES
Lyric by Johnny Mercer
Music by Harold Arlen

Ark. What did they do just when ev - 'ry - thing looked so

Outro-Verse

dark? "Man," they said, "We bet - ter ac - cent -

- tchu - ate the pos - i - tive, e - lim - i - nate the neg - a - tive, __

latch on to the af - firm - a - tive. Don't mess with Mis - ter In - be -

tween." No! Don't mess with Mis - ter In - be - tween.

Ain't Misbehavin'

from AIN'T MISBEHAVIN'
Words by Andy Razaf
Music by Thomas "Fats" Waller and Harry Brooks

All of Me

Words and Music by Seymour Simons and Gerald Marks

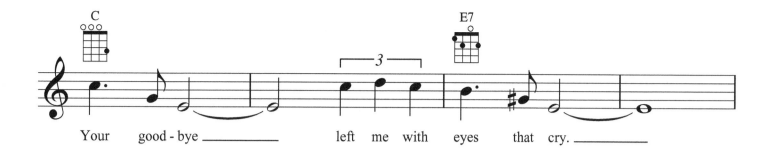

Your good - bye _____ left me with eyes that cry. _____

How can I _____ go on, dear, with - out you? _____

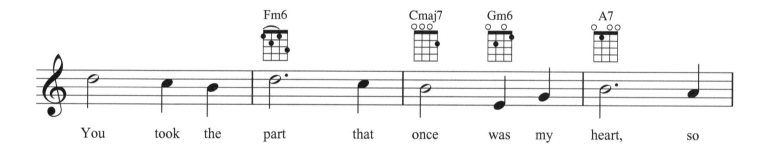

You took the part that once was my heart, so

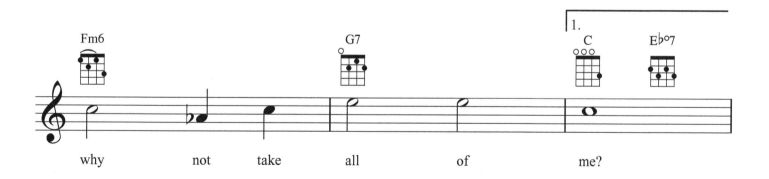

why not take all of me?

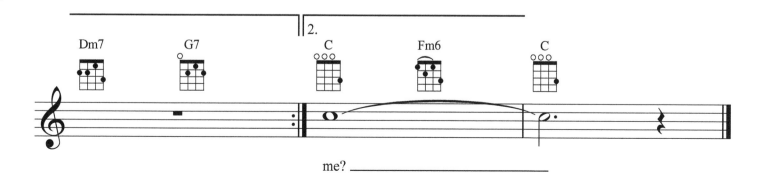

me? _____

As Time Goes By

from CASABLANCA

Words and Music by Herman Hupfeld

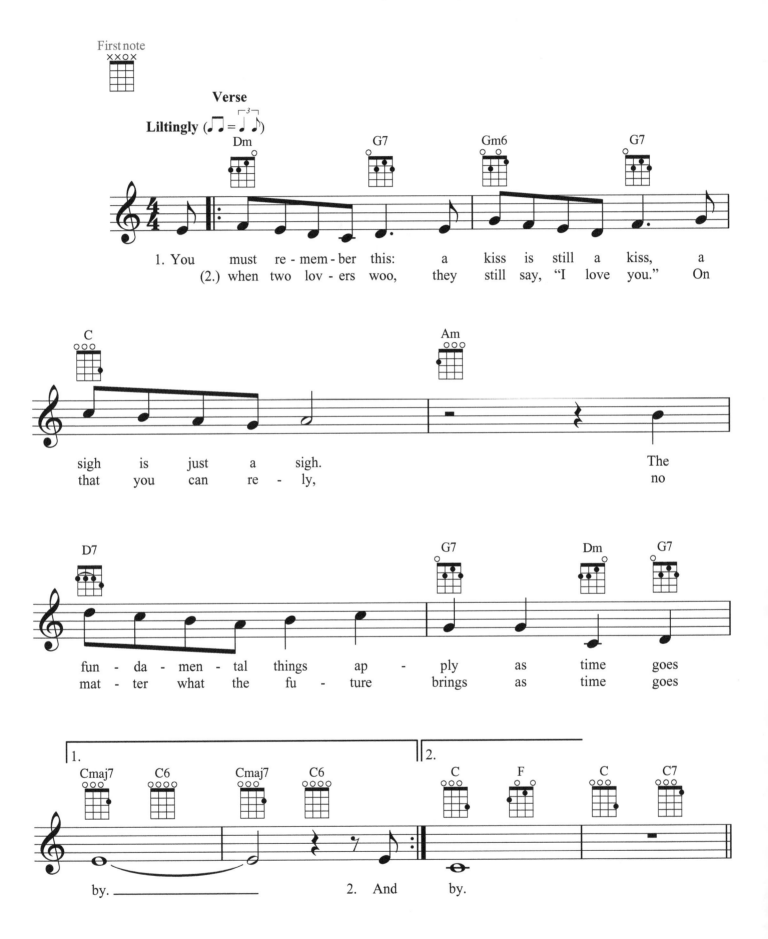

Autumn Leaves

English lyric by Johnny Mercer
French lyric by Jacques Prevert
Music by Joseph Kosma

I'll Take Romance

Lyrics by Oscar Hammerstein II
Music by Ben Oakland

mance. _____

Bridge

want   me,   call   me

in   the   hush   of   the   eve - ning.

When   you   call   me

in   the   hush   of   the   eve - ning,   I'll   rush   to   my

Outro-Verse

first real _____ ro - mance. _____ While my

heart   is   young   and   ea - ger   and   gay,

I'll   give   my   heart   a - way,   I'll   take   ro -

mance. _____ I'll   take   my

own _____ ro - mance. _____

Fly Me to the Moon
(In Other Words)

featured in the Motion Picture ONCE AROUND
Words and Music by Bart Howard

Verse
Medium Swing

1., 3. Fly me to the moon ____ and let me
2., 4. Fill my heart with song ____ and let me

play a - mong the stars. ____
sing for - ev - er - more. ____

Let me see what spring ____
You are all I long ____

____ is like on Ju - pi - ter and Mars. ____
____ for, all I wor - ship and a - dore. ____

____ In oth - er words, ____ hold my
____ In oth - er words, ____ please be

To Coda

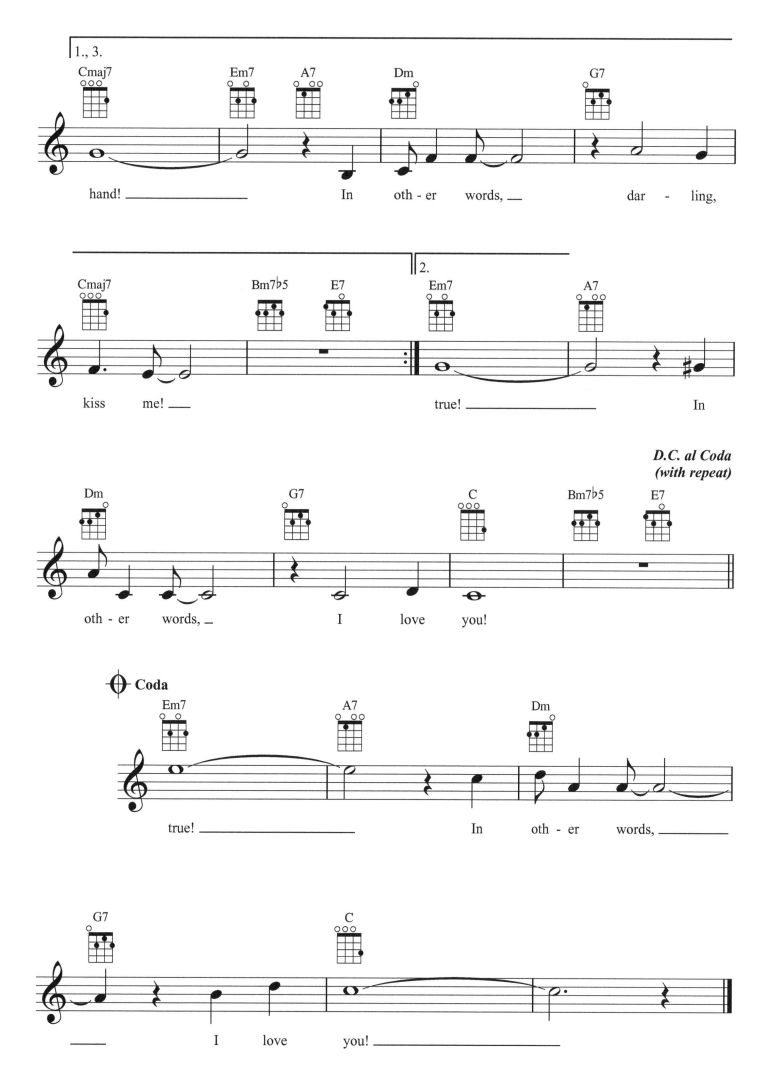

Honeysuckle Rose

from AIN'T MISBEHAVIN'
Words by Andy Razaf
Music by Thomas "Fats" Waller

How High the Moon

from TWO FOR THE SHOW
Lyrics by Nancy Hamilton
Music by Morgan Lewis

you. Some - where there's mu - sic; _____ it's where you

are. Some - where there's heav - en; _____

_____ how near, how far! The dark - est

night would shine if you would come ____ to me soon.

Un - til you will, how still my heart, how high the

1.
moon!

Some - where there's

2.
moon! _____

I'm Old Fashioned

from YOU WERE NEVER LOVELIER

Lyrics by Johnny Mercer
Music by Jerome Kern

Chorus
Liltingly, in 2

I'm old fash - ioned, I love the

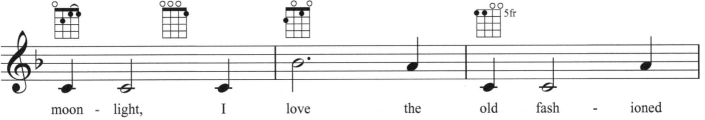

moon - light, I love the old fash - ioned

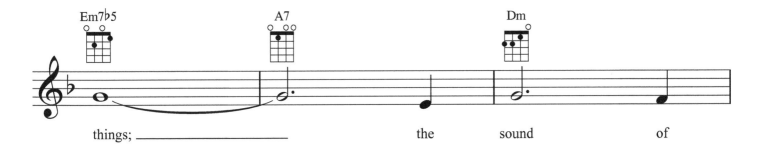

things; _____ the sound of

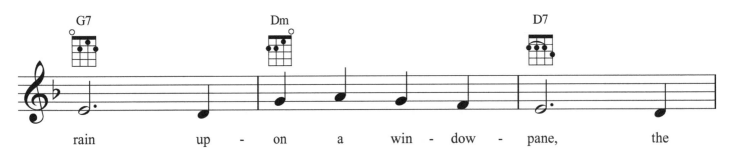

rain up - on a win - dow - pane, the

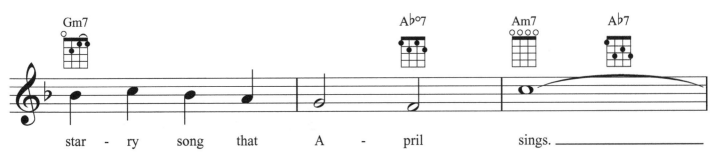

star - ry song that A - pril sings. _____

In a Sentimental Mood

Words and Music by Duke Ellington, Irving Mills and Manny Kurtz

Isn't It Romantic?

from the Paramount Picture LOVE ME TONIGHT

Words by Lorenz Hart
Music by Richard Rodgers

It's Only a Paper Moon

Lyric by Billy Rose and E.Y. "Yip" Harburg
Music by Harold Arlen

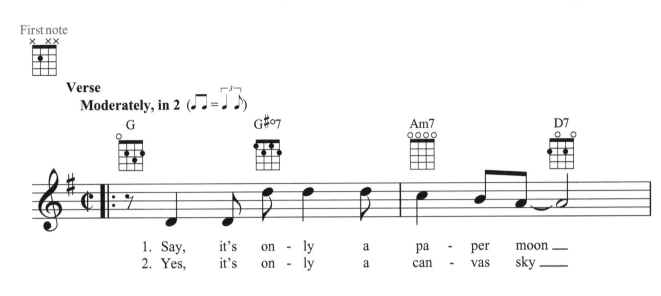

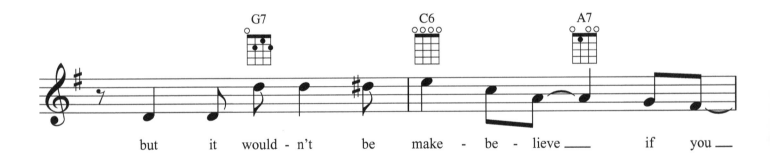

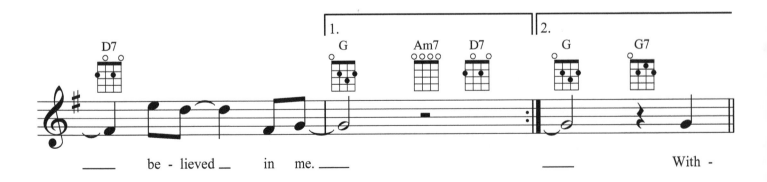

The Lady Is a Tramp

from BABES IN ARMS
Words by Lorenz Hart
Music by Richard Rodgers

That's why the la - dy is a tramp.

Bridge

1. | 2. |

I like the free, fresh

wind in my hair, _____ life with - out care. _____

Outro-Verse

I'm broke, _ it's oke. _ Hate Cal - i -

for - nia; it's cold and it's damp. _____

That's why the la - dy is a tramp. _____

Lulu's Back in Town

Words by Al Dubin
Music by Harry Warren

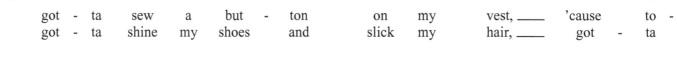

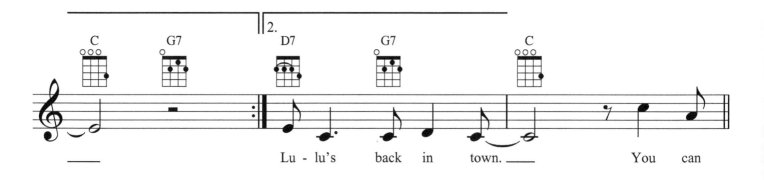

Bridge

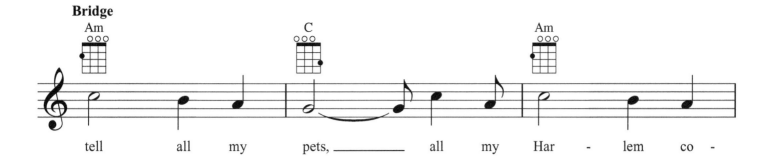

tell all my pets, _____ all my Har - lem co -

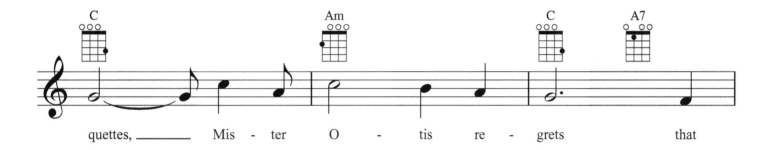

quettes, _____ Mis - ter O - tis re - grets that

Outro-Verse

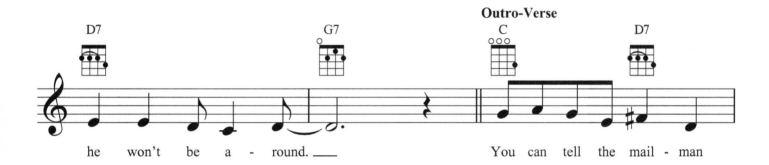

he won't be a - round. ___ You can tell the mail - man

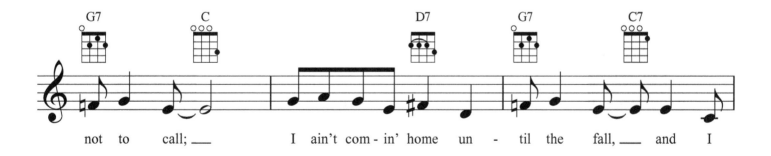

not to call; ___ I ain't com - in' home un - til the fall, ___ and I

might not get back home at all. ___ Lu - lu's back in town. ___

My Foolish Heart

Words by Ned Washington
Music by Victor Young

A Nightingale Sang in Berkeley Square

Lyric by Eric Maschwitz
Music by Manning Sherwin

* *Pronounced "Bar-kley"*

per - fect - ly will - ing to swear that when you turned and
mer - ry - go - round in a fair, for we were danc - ing

smiled at me, a night - in - gale sang in Ber - k'ley
cheek to cheek and a night - in - gale sang in Ber - k'ley

Bridge

Square.
Square.

The moon that lin - gered o - ver
When dawn came steal - ing up all

Lon - don town, __ poor puz - zled moon, he wore a frown.
gold and blue __ to in - ter - rupt our ren - dez - vous,

How could he know we two were so in love? __ The whole damn world seemed
I still re - mem - ber how you smiled and said, __ "Was that a dream or

Outro-Verse

up - side down. The streets of town were paved with stars; it was
was it true?" Our home - ward step was just as light as the

such a ro - man - tic af - fair. And as we kissed and
tap - danc - ing feet of As - taire. And like an ech - o

said "good- night," a night - in - gale sang in Ber - k'ley Square. ____
far a - way, a night - in - gale sang in Ber - k'ley

____ 2. How Square. I know 'cause I was

there, that night in Ber - k'ley Square. ____

Smile

Theme from MODERN TIMES
Words by John Turner and Geoffrey Parsons
Music by Charles Chaplin

On the Sunny Side of the Street

Lyric by Dorothy Fields
Music by Jimmy McHugh

First note

Verse
Moderately, in 2

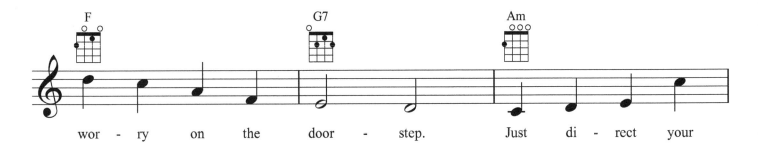

1. Grab your coat and get your hat, leave your

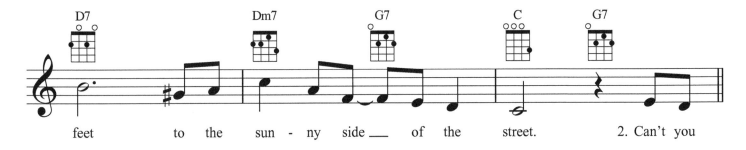

wor - ry on the door - step. Just di - rect your

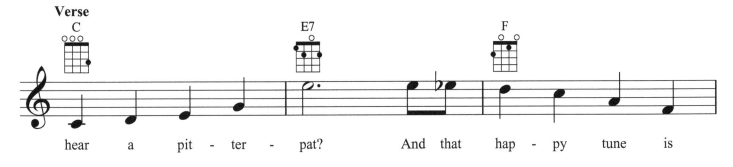

feet to the sun - ny side ___ of the street. 2. Can't you

Verse

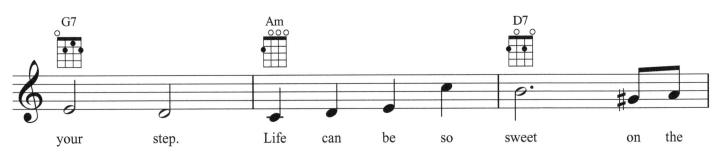

hear a pit - ter - pat? And that hap - py tune is

your step. Life can be so sweet on the

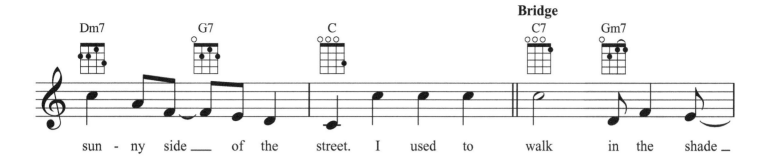

sun - ny side ___ of the street. I used to walk in the shade ___

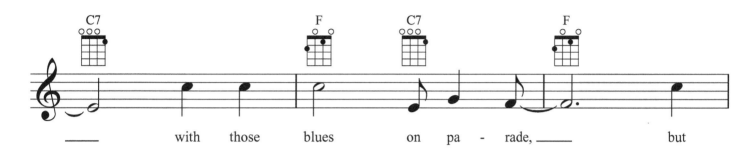

___ with those blues on pa - rade, ___ but

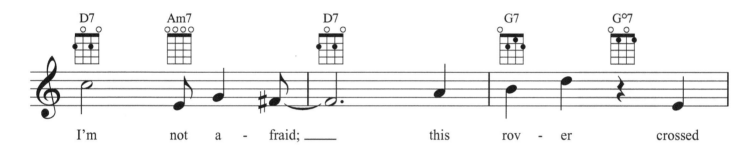

I'm not a - fraid; ___ this rov - er crossed

Outro-Verse

o - ver. If I nev - er have a cent, I'll be

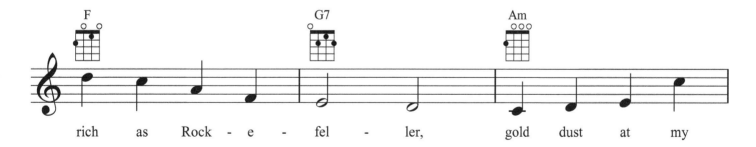

rich as Rock - e - fel - ler, gold dust at my

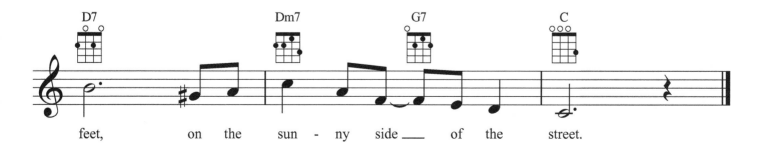

feet, on the sun - ny side ___ of the street.

'S Wonderful

from FUNNY FACE

Music and Lyrics by George Gershwin and Ira Gershwin

Stompin' at the Savoy

Words by Andy Razaf
Music by Benny Goodman, Edgar Sampson and Chick Webb

Summertime

from *PORGY AND BESS*®

Music and Lyrics by George Gershwin, DuBose and Dorothy Heyward and Ira Gershwin

Sweet Lorraine

Words by Mitchell Parish
Music by Cliff Burwell

miss the sun, for it's in my sweet-ie's smile. ___

Just to think that I'm the luck-y one who will lead her down the aisle. ___

Outro-Verse

___ Each night I pray that no-bod-y steals her

heart a - way. Just can't wait un-til that hap-py day

when I mar-ry sweet Lor - raine. ___

Tangerine

from the Paramount Picture THE FLEET'S IN
Words by Johnny Mercer
Music by Victor Schertzinger

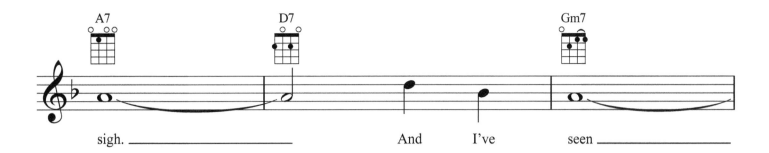

sigh. _____ And I've seen _____

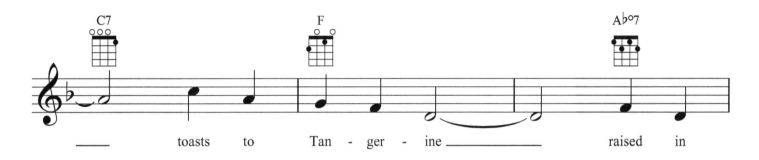

____ toasts to Tan - ger - ine _____ raised in

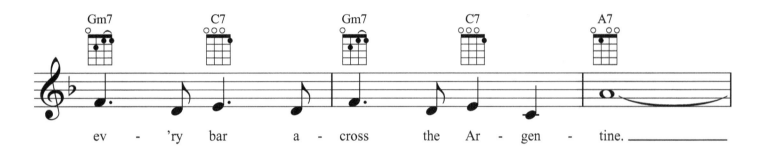

ev - 'ry bar a - cross the Ar - gen - tine. _____

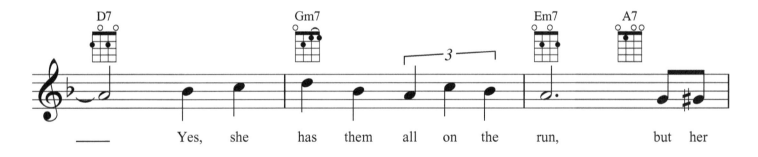

____ Yes, she has them all on the run, but her

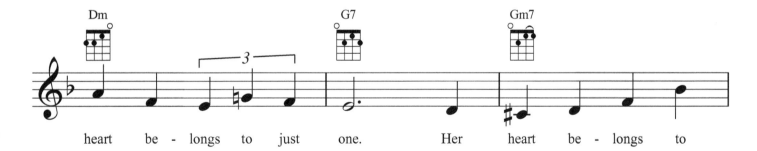

heart be - longs to just one. Her heart be - longs to

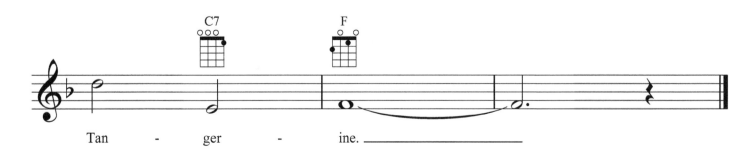

Tan - ger - ine. _____

What'll I Do?

from MUSIC BOX REVUE OF 1924
Words and Music by Irving Berlin

What-'ll I do when you are far a-way and I am blue? What-'ll I do?

What-'ll I do when I am won-d'ring who is kiss-ing you? What-'ll I do?

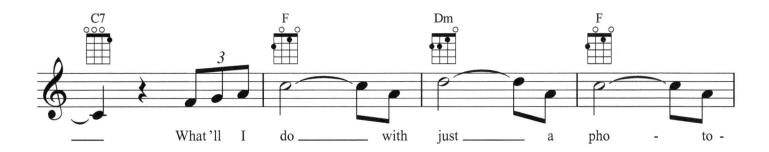

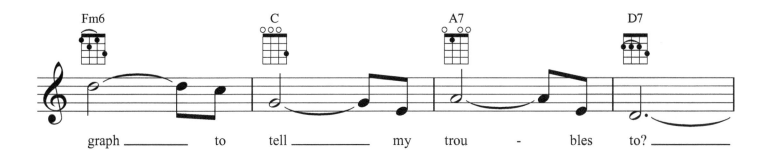

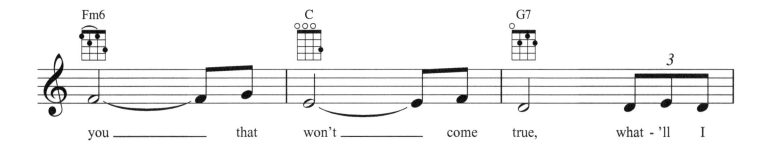

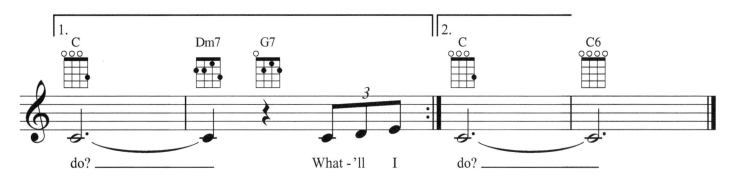

The Best Collections for Ukulele

The Best Songs Ever

70 songs have now been arranged for ukulele. Includes: Always • Bohemian Rhapsody • Memory • My Favorite Things • Over the Rainbow • Piano Man • What a Wonderful World • Yesterday • You Raise Me Up • and more.

00282413.......$17.99

Campfire Songs for Ukulele

30 favorites to sing as you roast marshmallows and strum your uke around the campfire. Includes: God Bless the U.S.A. • Hallelujah • The House of the Rising Sun • I Walk the Line • Puff the Magic Dragon • Wagon Wheel • You Are My Sunshine • and more.

00129170 ....$14.99

The Daily Ukulele

arr. Liz and Jim Beloff
Strum a different song everyday with easy arrangements of 365 of your favorite songs in one big songbook! Includes favorites by the Beatles, Beach Boys, and Bob Dylan, folk songs, pop songs, kids' songs, Christmas carols, and Broadway and Hollywood tunes, all with a spiral binding for ease of use.

00240356 Original Edition.................$39.99
00240681 Leap Year Edition $39.99
00119270 Portable Edition $37.50

Disney Hits for Ukulele

Play 23 of your favorite Disney songs on your ukulele. Includes: The Bare Necessities • Cruella De Vil • Do You Want to Build a Snowman? • Kiss the Girl • Lava • Let It Go • Once upon a Dream • A Whole New World • and more.

00151250 ....$16.99

Also available:
00291547 **Disney Fun Songs for Ukulele** ...$16.99
00701708 **Disney Songs for Ukulele**.......$14.99
00334696 **First 50 Disney Songs on Ukulele** .$16.99

First 50 Songs You Should Play on Ukulele

An amazing collec-tion of 50 accessible, must-know favorites: Edelweiss • Hey, Soul Sister • I Walk the Line • I'm Yours • Imagine • Over the Rainbow • Peaceful Easy Feeling • The Rainbow Connection • Riptide • more.

00149250 ....$16.99

Also available:
00292082 **First 50 Melodies on Ukulele** ...$15.99
00289029 **First 50 Songs on Solo Ukulele**..$15.99
00347437 **First 50 Songs to Strum on Uke** .$16.99

40 Most Streamed Songs for Ukulele

40 top hits that sound great on uke! Includes: Despacito • Feel It Still • Girls like You • Happier • Havana • High Hopes • The Middle • Perfect • 7 Rings • Shallow • Shape of You • Something Just like This • Stay • Sucker • Sunflower • Sweet but Psycho • Thank U, Next • There's Nothing Holdin' Me Back • Without Me • and more!

00298113 ....$17.99

The 4 Chord Songbook

With just 4 chords, you can play 50 hot songs on your ukulele! Songs include: Brown Eyed Girl • Do Wah Diddy Diddy • Hey Ya! • Ho Hey • Jessie's Girl • Let It Be • One Love • Stand by Me • Toes • With or Without You • and many more.

00142050.......$16.99

Also available:
00141143 **The 3-Chord Songbook**.........$16.99

Pop Songs for Kids

30 easy pop favorites for kids to play on uke, including: Brave • Can't Stop the Feeling! • Feel It Still • Fight Song • Happy • Havana • House of Gold • How Far I'll Go • Let It Go • Remember Me (Ernesto de la Cruz) • Rewrite the Stars • Roar • Shake It Off • Story of My Life • What Makes You Beautiful • and more.

00284415 ....$16.99

Simple Songs for Ukulele

50 favorites for standard G-C-E-A ukulele tuning, including: All Along the Watchtower • Can't Help Falling in Love • Don't Worry, Be Happy • Ho Hey • I'm Yours • King of the Road • Sweet Home Alabama • You Are My Sunshine • and more.

00156815........$14.99

Also available:
00276644 **More Simple Songs for Ukulele** .$14.99

Top Hits of 2020

18 uke-friendly tunes of 2020 are featured in this collection of melody, lyric and chord arrangements in standard G-C-E-A tuning. Includes: Adore You (Harry Styles) • Before You Go (Lewis Capaldi) • Cardigan (Taylor Swift) • Daisies (Katy Perry) • I Dare You (Kelly Clarkson) • Level of Concern (twenty one pilots) • No Time to Die (Billie Eilish) • Rain on Me (Lady Gaga feat. Ariana Grande) • Say So (Doja Cat) • and more.

00355553 ....$14.99

Also available:
00302274 **Top Hits of 2019** $14.99

Ukulele: The Most Requested Songs

Strum & Sing Series
Cherry Lane Music
Nearly 50 favorites all expertly arranged for ukulele! Includes: Bubbly • Build Me Up, Buttercup • Cecilia • Georgia on My Mind • Kokomo • L-O-V-E • Your Body Is a Wonderland • and more.

02501453 ....$14.99

The Ultimate Ukulele Fake Book

Uke enthusiasts will love this giant, spiral-bound collection of over 400 songs for uke! Includes: Crazy • Dancing Queen • Downtown • Fields of Gold • Happy • Hey Jude • 7 Years • Summertime • Thinking Out Loud • Thriller • Wagon Wheel • and more.

00175500 9" x 12" Edition $45.00
00319997 5.5" x 8.5" Edition $39.99

Order today from your favorite music retailer at
halleonard.com

Prices, contents and availability subject to change without notice

Disney characters and artwork TM & © 2021 Disney

0621
479

UKULELE ENSEMBLE SERIES

The songs in these collections are playable by any combination of ukuleles (soprano, concert, tenor or baritone). Each arrangement features the melody, a harmony part, and a "bass" line. Chord symbols are also provided if you wish to add a rhythm part. For groups with more than three or four ukuleles, the parts may be doubled.

CHRISTMAS CAROLS
Early Intermediate Level

Away in a Manger • Carol of the Bells • Deck the Hall • The First Noel • God Rest Ye Merry, Gentlemen • Hark! the Herald Angels Sing • It Came Upon the Midnight Clear • Jingle Bells • Joy to the World • O Christmas Tree • O Come, All Ye Faithful • O Holy Night • O Little Town of Bethlehem • Silent Night • Up on the Housetop.
00129248 .... $9.99

CHRISTMAS SONGS
Early Intermediate Level

The Chipmunk Song • The Christmas Song (Chestnuts Roasting on an Open Fire) • Do You Hear What I Hear • Feliz Navidad • Frosty the Snow Man • Have Yourself a Merry Little Christmas • Here Comes Santa Claus (Right Down Santa Claus Lane) • A Holly Jolly Christmas • (There's No Place Like) Home for the Holidays • Jingle Bell Rock • The Little Drummer Boy • Merry Christmas, Darling • The Most Wonderful Time of the Year • Silver Bells • White Christmas.
00129247 .... $9.99

CLASSIC ROCK
Mid-Intermediate Level

Aqualung • Behind Blue Eyes • Born to Be Wild • Crazy Train • Fly Like an Eagle • Free Bird • Hey Jude • Low Rider • Moondance • Oye Como Va • Proud Mary • (I Can't Get No) Satisfaction • Smoke on the Water • Summertime Blues • Sunshine of Your Love.
00103904 .... $9.99

DISNEY FAVORITES
Early Intermediate Level

The Bare Necessities • Beauty and the Beast • Can You Feel the Love Tonight • Colors of the Wind • A Dream Is a Wish Your Heart Makes • It's a Small World • Let It Go • Let's Go Fly a Kite • Little April Shower • Mickey Mouse March • Seize the Day • The Siamese Cat Song • Supercalifragilisticexpialidocious • Under the Sea • A Whole New World.
00279513 .... $9.99

HAWAIIAN SONGS
Mid-Intermediate Level

Aloha Oe • Beyond the Rainbow • Harbor Lights • Hawaiian War Chant (Ta-Hu-Wa-Hu-Wai) • The Hawaiian Wedding Song (Ke Kali Nei Au) • Ka-lu-a • Lovely Hula Hands • Mele Kalikimaka • The Moon of Manakoora • One Paddle, Two Paddle • Pearly Shells (Pupu 'O 'Ewa) • Red Sails in the Sunset • Sleepy Lagoon • Song of the Islands • Tiny Bubbles.
00119254 .... $9.99

THE NUTCRACKER
Late Intermediate Level

Arabian Dance ("Coffee") • Chinese Dance ("Tea") • Dance of the Reed-Flutes • Dance of the Sugar Plum Fairy • March • Overture • Russian Dance ("Trepak") • Waltz of the Flowers.
00119908 .... $9.99

ROCK INSTRUMENTALS
Late Intermediate Level

Beck's Bolero • Cissy Strut • Europa (Earth's Cry Heaven's Smile) • Frankenstein • Green Onions • Jessica • Misirlou • Perfidia • Pick Up the Pieces • Pipeline • Rebel 'Rouser • Sleepwalk • Tequila • Walk Don't Run • Wipe Out.
00103909 .... $9.99

STANDARDS & GEMS
Mid-Intermediate Level

Autumn Leaves • Cheek to Cheek • Easy to Love • Fly Me to the Moon • I Only Have Eyes for You • It Had to Be You • Laura • Mack the Knife • My Funny Valentine • Theme from "New York, New York" • Over the Rainbow • Satin Doll • Some Day My Prince Will Come • Summertime • The Way You Look Tonight.
00103898 .... $9.99

THEME MUSIC
Mid-Intermediate Level

Batman Theme • Theme from E.T. (The Extra-Terrestrial) • Forrest Gump – Main Title (Feather Theme) • The Godfather (Love Theme) • Hawaii Five-O Theme • He's a Pirate • Linus and Lucy • Mission: Impossible Theme • Peter Gunn • The Pink Panther • Raiders March • (Ghost) Riders in the Sky (A Cowboy Legend) • Theme from Spider Man • Theme from "Star Trek®" • Theme from "Superman."
00103903 .... $9.99

HAL•LEONARD®
UKULELE PLAY-ALONG

Now you can play your favorite songs on your uke with great-sounding backing tracks to help you sound like a bona fide pro! The audio also features playback tools so you can adjust the tempo without changing the pitch and loop challenging parts.

1. POP HITS
00701451 Book/CD Pack $15.99

3. HAWAIIAN FAVORITES
00701453 Book/Online Audio $14.99

4. CHILDREN'S SONGS
00701454 Book/Online Audio $14.99

5. CHRISTMAS SONGS
00701696 Book/CD Pack $12.99

6. LENNON & MCCARTNEY
00701723 Book/Online Audio $12.99

7. DISNEY FAVORITES
00701724 Book/Online Audio $14.99

8. CHART HITS
00701745 Book/CD Pack $15.99

9. THE SOUND OF MUSIC
00701784 Book/CD Pack $14.99

10. MOTOWN
00701964 Book/CD Pack $12.99

11. CHRISTMAS STRUMMING
00702458 Book/Online Audio $12.99

12. BLUEGRASS FAVORITES
00702584 Book/CD Pack $12.99

13. UKULELE SONGS
00702599 Book/CD Pack $12.99

14. JOHNNY CASH
00702615 Book/Online Audio $15.99

15. COUNTRY CLASSICS
00702834 Book/CD Pack $12.99

16. STANDARDS
00702835 Book/CD Pack $12.99

17. POP STANDARDS
00702836 Book/CD Pack $12.99

18. IRISH SONGS
00703086 Book/Online Audio $12.99

19. BLUES STANDARDS
00703087 Book/CD Pack $12.99

20. FOLK POP ROCK
00703088 Book/CD Pack $12.99

21. HAWAIIAN CLASSICS
00703097 Book/CD Pack $12.99

22. ISLAND SONGS
00703098 Book/CD Pack $12.99

23. TAYLOR SWIFT
00221966 Book/Online Audio $16.99

24. WINTER WONDERLAND
00101871 Book/CD Pack $12.99

25. GREEN DAY
00110398 Book/CD Pack $14.99

26. BOB MARLEY
00110399 Book/Online Audio $14.99

27. TIN PAN ALLEY
00116358 Book/CD Pack $12.99

28. STEVIE WONDER
00116736 Book/CD Pack $14.99

29. OVER THE RAINBOW & OTHER FAVORITES
00117076 Book/Online Audio $15.99

30. ACOUSTIC SONGS
00122336 Book/CD Pack $14.99

31. JASON MRAZ
00124166 Book/CD Pack $14.99

32. TOP DOWNLOADS
00127507 Book/CD Pack $14.99

33. CLASSICAL THEMES
00127892 Book/Online Audio $14.99

34. CHRISTMAS HITS
00128602 Book/CD Pack $14.99

35. SONGS FOR BEGINNERS
00129009 Book/Online Audio $14.99

36. ELVIS PRESLEY HAWAII
00138199 Book/Online Audio $14.99

37. LATIN
00141191 Book/Online Audio $14.99

38. JAZZ
00141192 Book/Online Audio $14.99

39. GYPSY JAZZ
00146559 Book/Online Audio $15.99

40. TODAY'S HITS
00160845 Book/Online Audio $14.99

HAL•LEONARD®
www.halleonard.com